the CMMRD book
a mismatch memoir and guide

sam alexandra rose

Foreword by Lynn Dunne,
CEO of Bowel Research UK

Edited by Christopher John Eggett

ISBN: 9798853249370

www.writersam.co.uk

twitter.com/writersamr

Copyright © Sam Alexandra Rose 2023

Peeking Cat Literary

Also by this author

Gut Feelings:
Coping with Cancer and Living with Lynch Syndrome
memoir

collected quirks
poetry collection

Empowerthy
poetry chapbook

Contents

Foreword

What a pleasure to be asked to write a foreword for Sam's book. Her book is timely as we hear more and more about the role of genomics in medicine and head towards personalised developments in medical care that couldn't have been imagined a few years ago. Genomics is baffling for most of us and that is where books like this are such an incredible gift.

Anyone who has received a cancer diagnosis goes on a rollercoaster journey that includes living with the occasionally recurring thought "has it come back?" when feeling tired or unwell. For those with a diagnosis of Lynch syndrome or CMMRD, the stakes are much higher and that recurring thought is a daily, frightening one. Sam's book is good medicine for those thoughts.

Sam writes with the humour and honesty that only someone who has been through the mill of three cancer journeys can; she will have you laughing on one page and crying on the next. Her explanations are clear and helpful, particularly for someone who has just been diagnosed with Lynch syndrome or CMMRD or is supporting someone with the same. It is a humane and helpful navigation of a difficult subject for a difficult journey.

This book is a non-medical person's true north guide through Lynch syndrome and CMMRD written by someone I am privileged to know who really is one in a million.

Lynn Dunne, MA, RGN, RCNT
CEO of Bowel Research UK

Prologue

As far as I can tell from my research, this is the first book on CMMRD. A search of Amazon and the British Library returns nothing, and Google only provides websites and scientific journals. In terms of books, there is nothing for patients, families, or those who may benefit from an introduction to the subject. This is the book that would have been helpful for me when I was diagnosed with CMMRD. Part memoir, part helpful guide, this is about how I have accepted my diagnosis and am beating the odds at the age of thirty-five.

Since CMMRD often affects children, it is worth noting that this book is not written about children specifically or from the point of view of a parent. It is from my point of view as an adult with CMMRD living in the UK. It is about coming to terms, finding acceptance, and experiencing my three cancer diagnoses and surgeries that have come with this genetic condition. Other people will have had different experiences with CMMRD and it may help to read those stories too where you can find them.

In this book, I refer to CMMRD as a rare condition. I don't consider it to be a disease as such, but it can cause disease. It is an ultra-rare inherited genetic condition that affects very few people. But although there are not many people with CMMRD, there are over 6,000 known rare diseases in the world and 1 in 17 people will be affected by a rare disease at some point in their lives – that's over 3.5 million people in the UK and

30 million across the whole of Europe.[1] So while there are very few people affected by each individual rare condition, there are a lot of people with rare diseases, and we all matter. CMMRD may be rare, but everyone I know has met someone who has it. This is a story of denial and acceptance from one ultra-rare adult living with CMMRD.

There is no scientific mumbo jumbo, there are no scary predictions of life expectancy. There are only facts, thoughts and feelings from someone who has made it to adulthood with CMMRD. Oh, and poetry. I am a writer after all, not just of memoir and non-fiction. I have been a writer all my life and my experiences are therefore punctuated with a poem for every chapter, and a few writing references thrown in for good measure.

And there is hope. This book is for anyone who has had a CMMRD diagnosis, and for parents of children with a CMMRD diagnosis and who may be worried about the length and quality of life for their child. It's for clinicians who want – and need – to know more about rare conditions and what it's like for patients to live with increased cancer risk. And it's for the general public interested in ultra-rare disorders. I hope you find hope in these pages.

---

[1] 'What Is a Rare Disease? - Rare Disease UK', 12 April 2018, https://www.raredisease.org.uk/what-is-a-rare-disease/.

Coming To Terms
Written on Saturday 28th May, 2022 at 10:39

I am "coming to terms" with the diagnosis I received
over ten years ago
years later I'm still trying to think it through
like what is "coming to terms" anyway?
what and where are the terms and how do we get there
or come to them

why can't the terms come to me
why do I have to do all the hard work

can't I get the terms sent to my house?
they deliver everything these days
Deliveroo, Uber Eats, those little robots I see trying to
cross the road
I helped one of them up a kerb once and it thanked me
surely the terms would have fit in his little food
compartment

I'm an Amazon Prime member, you're saying they won't
deliver the terms to me?

yes I'm lazy
and I know I'm skirting around the issue
and not actually addressing the thing I apparently need
to come to terms with

one day I will find all the right terms to describe this
issue
and maybe by then someone will have created a
company

called Uber Terms or Prime Terms

tasty terms, straight to your door
pay more for priority delivery
track your rider on the map

I hope they're in a car and not on a bike
or the size of the terms I've ordered
makes me fear for their safety

What is CMMRD?

I am one in a million. That's not me being conceited; I literally am. While rare conditions are those that affect less than one in 2,000 people, ultra-rare conditions affect one in 50,000. This puts CMMRD in a league of its own as it affects an estimated one in a million patients.[2] That's right, I'm one in a million – you heard it here first. (Except you perhaps didn't as I use that line all the time.) In fact, as my partner was quick to research, those odds are somewhere between getting five numbers and five numbers and a bonus ball on the National Lottery.[3]

But what is CMMRD? It stands for Constitutional Mismatch Repair Deficiency and it's a genetic condition that increases a person's risk of getting different types of cancer. It is related to another genetic condition called Lynch syndrome, which also increases cancer risk. But while Lynch syndrome occurs when a person inherits faulty genes from one parent, CMMRD occurs when both parents have Lynch syndrome and the person inherits faulty genes from both parents. To understand how CMMRD is inherited, let's first explain Lynch syndrome further.

---

[2] Malak Abedalthagafi, 'Constitutional Mismatch Repair-Deficiency: Current Problems and Emerging Therapeutic Strategies', Oncotarget 9, no. 83 (23 October 2018): 35458–69, https://doi.org/10.18632/oncotarget.26249.
[3] 'Lotto Online Game Procedures', The National Lottery, https://www.national-lottery.co.uk/games/lotto/game-procedures.

Mismatch Repair Genes: The Editors of Our Bodies' Books

Lynch syndrome is a genetic condition that increases a person's cancer risk. It used to be known as hereditary non-polyposis colorectal cancer (HNPCC). People with Lynch syndrome have an up to 80% risk of getting bowel cancer. It can also increase the risk of getting gynaecological, stomach, kidney, liver, skin and brain cancer, depending on which of your genes are affected. The genes are called MLH1, MSH2, MSH6, PMS2, and EPCAM, and if you have Lynch syndrome in the family you may have come across these names. These are mismatch repair (MMR) genes.

Mismatch repair genes repair mistakes that occur during DNA replication. As they look for mistakes and correct them, I like to think of these genes as the editors or proofreaders of our bodies. Imagine a tiny person sitting at a desk inside your body, with stacks of paper piled high in front of them. That person is your editor, your mismatch repair gene. And the paper is the DNA that needs to be checked. The editor takes their red pen and corrects all of the mistakes. For a real editor, these might be spelling errors, grammatical errors, inconsistencies or incorrect facts. Mismatch repair genes, the editors of your DNA, will be correcting mistakes in DNA replication that could otherwise lead to cancer if left uncorrected. Of course, for a real editor, the stakes are not very high – a spelling mistake in a book or newspaper isn't a matter of life or death. Mistakes in DNA, however, can be catastrophic. This is why your MMR genes are so important. The editor finishes the corrections and the paper is taken away so that the printed publication can be finished correctly – or so that your DNA can be repaired and all is well.

Because they repair DNA, mismatch repair genes help prevent us from getting cancer, which I suppose in this metaphor is the worst possible grammatical error (even worse than mixing up your and you're). Lynch syndrome is when these mismatch repair genes or editors are "broken" due to alterations or mutations, so they don't do their job properly. Imagine the editor's desk is empty, or they are sleeping at their desk, or making paper aeroplanes instead of working. However you think of it, the editor or MMR gene is not doing its job – leaving mistakes uncorrected and increasing cancer risk.

This diagram may help explain how genes related to Lynch syndrome are passed on in families:

We each inherit two copies of each gene from our parents. You can see this in the diagram – the ticks represent normal genes and the crosses represent mutated genes. So if your mother has Lynch syndrome (in other words, one of her two copies of the gene has a mutation) and your father does not have Lynch syndrome, you might inherit a normal gene from each parent and not have Lynch syndrome, like the boy on the left. Or you might inherit your mother's mutated gene and also have Lynch syndrome, like the other two children. The chances of getting Lynch syndrome if one parent has it are 50%.

It's worth noting here that Lynch syndrome itself is not rare. It's estimated that 1 in 400 people in the UK have Lynch syndrome, but only 5% know they have it.[4] The other 95% are wandering around oblivious to their increased cancer risk, though with an increased focus on genetic screening, it is hoped the tide is changing on this.

CMMRD: "Double" Lynch Syndrome

Now that we understand Lynch syndrome, we can explain what CMMRD is by thinking again about families and how these problems with the genes are passed on. We've talked about what could happen if one parent has Lynch syndrome. But what if they both have

---

[4] 'NHS England » Life-Saving NHS Test Helping to Diagnose Thousands with Cancer-Causing Syndrome', https://www.england.nhs.uk/2023/04/life-saving-nhs-test-helping-to-diagnose-thousands-with-cancer-causing-syndrome.

it, like mine? The mother has one normal gene and one with a mutation. So does the father. The child might therefore inherit the mother's normal gene and the father's normal gene and not have Lynch syndrome at all. This is what happened with my sister – great news, as this meant she didn't pass it onto her children. Or the child might have inherited the mother's normal gene and the father's mutated gene, or the mother's mutated gene and the father's normal gene. This would mean they have one normal gene and one mutation, and would therefore have Lynch syndrome. Finally, there are those who inherit their mother's mutated gene *and* their father's mutated gene. Like me. And like my brother, who died from a brain tumour at age sixteen when I was one year old. These people have CMMRD, or Constitutional Mismatch Repair Deficiency. It's also known as Biallelic Mismatch Repair Deficiency or BMMRD. You can see the diagram of children inheriting CMMRD, Lynch, or neither on the next page. If Lynch syndrome increases cancer risk, what I often refer to as "double Lynch syndrome" increases it even more. CMMRD increases the risk of cancer including bowel, brain, and blood cancer such as leukaemia or non-Hodgkin lymphoma.

CMMRD almost always results in childhood or early adult cancer. Nearly everyone with CMMRD gets cancer before the age of eighteen.[5] The average age for getting cancer with CMMRD is just seven and a half years old.[6] At the age of thirty-five, I feel like I'm beating the odds pretty well - though I've had three different types of cancer so far.

---

[5] 'Constitutional Mismatch Repair Deficiency Syndrome: MedlinePlus Genetics', https://medlineplus.gov/genetics/condition/constitutional-mismatch-repair-deficiency-syndrome/.
[6] 'Constitutional Mismatch Repair Deficiency', https://www.genturis.eu/l=eng/Thematic-disease-groups/Other-rare-genturis/Constitutional-Mismatch-Repair-Deficiency.html.

Aside from the cancer risk, people with CMMRD may have changes in skin colouring – patches of skin or spots that are darker than the surrounding area, known as café-au-lait spots. Sometimes they may have lighter patches of skin or freckling. Some also have Lisch nodules, which are benign growths in the iris that don't affect the person's vision.[7]

There is no cure for CMMRD and no treatment other than regular screening and the subsequent treatment of any cancers that may develop. As it is so rare, not much is known about CMMRD at the moment and the guidelines around recommended screening are often updated to take the latest research and findings into consideration.

Denial: The Longest River in this Book

With all that scary science and statistics to look into, you can perhaps understand why I didn't write this book sooner. This is the book I might have published under different circumstances in 2021. This book is partially about denial and eventual acceptance, and how those things came to be. In January 2019 while recovering from Whipple surgery, I wrote the bulk of my memoir *Gut Feelings: Coping with Cancer and Living with Lynch Syndrome* – 50,000 words in ten days. It was a

---

[7] Katharina Wimmer et al., 'Diagnostic Criteria for Constitutional Mismatch Repair Deficiency Syndrome: Suggestions of the European Consortium "Care for CMMRD" (C4CMMRD)', Journal of Medical Genetics 51, no. 6 (1 June 2014): 355–65, https://doi.org/10.1136/jmedgenet-2014-102284.

very difficult book to write because it was a memoir of my cancer experiences from 2010 to 2019, and it was equally difficult to edit as it was a constant revisiting of those hard times. I periodically returned to the book to edit it and even submitted it to a publisher, who requested the whole thing after seeing the first three chapters but didn't take it further than that. Eventually, in early 2021 I edited the book to a state I was happy with, created a front cover and blurb, and started selling it through Amazon.

This was a book about cancer, about Lynch syndrome. It did not mention CMMRD by name anywhere. Why? Because ten years after my diagnosis, I still couldn't bear thinking about my horribly increased cancer risk. It was too scary. It had taken about half that time just for me to think about Lynch syndrome without freaking out. So this is the book I would have written about CMMRD. It even appears to be the first book anyone has ever written about CMMRD. It addresses what I could not address sooner, and tells the story of how I got to this place of acceptance.

My Cancer Stories In Brief(ish)

your body will betray you
Written on Wednesday 31st January, 2018 at 22:45

your body doesn't care
that it's nearly Christmas
your body doesn't care
about your birthday
your body will betray you
without checking the calendar

There was no indication of CMMRD when I was a child. I had a very unremarkable medical record until the age of 22, when in January 2010 late at night, my bottom started bleeding after I went to the toilet and it wouldn't stop. I thought it was haemorrhoids so in the morning my parents took me to the GP, who didn't know what it was and sent me to A&E with a referral. The doctor at A&E said there was a little polyp that had stuck its head out and was bleeding. I had to have four units of blood put back in me so stayed overnight. In the morning, I met Mr Rashed, who would be my trusted colorectal consultant for the next ten years.

The next few months are a hazy memory but involved a CT, MRI and a very painful colonoscopy where lots of polyps were identified. In May I found out some were cancerous. I was 22 years old and being told I needed to have my bowel removed and a stoma created. My parents and I didn't even know what a stoma was. For anyone else who doesn't, it's an opening on the abdomen where urine, or in this case poo, comes out. You may have heard of people wearing colostomy bags to collect poo. I was going to have an ileostomy, which is very similar. An ileostomy is when the last part of the small intestine is connected to the abdominal wall (as opposed to part of the large bowel being connected to the abdomen, in the case of a colostomy). The stoma nurses gave me a bag of leaflets and a sponge stoma to show me what it was like, which sat in the corner of the dining room untouched. I suppose that was the beginning of not wanting to know. I had my bowel removed on 27th July 2010, with a view to reversing it and having an internal pouch created a few months later. I was in hospital for days before I even looked at my stoma. When I came

19

home, I think it was easier to deal with the ileostomy bag every day because I knew it was only going to be temporary, and my mum helped me a lot with it. In January 2011, I had the reversal operation. A makeshift large intestine was made from part of my small intestine to form an internal pouch or J-pouch. I did worry I had made the wrong decision when I wasn't keeping food down in the hospital and was pooping seventeen times a day, but it settled down and my pouch and I have living together in harmony since then, apart from the occasional nighttime leakage caused by too much delicious cheese.

Because I was so young when the polyps were found and I was diagnosed with bowel cancer, my parents and I were sent for genetic testing. This happened in September 2011 and we found out that my parents both had Lynch syndrome and I had CMMRD. I'll cover genetic testing in more detail in the next chapter. The CMMRD diagnosis meant I was put on a screening programme that has developed over the years. Typically, I would have a CT scan every year for five years after surgery. Sometimes this also results in an MRI if something needs to be looked at more closely. I also have a regular flexible sigmoidoscopy, which is similar to a colonoscopy but takes only ten minutes or so and looks at a smaller area. After all, you can't have a colonoscopy if you don't have a colon. I also have regular gastroscopies, which is when they put a camera down your throat and into your stomach, and in my opinion that is the worst one. I'll go into more detail about these tests later. In the beginning, those were the only tests I remember having. But this was going to change.

I plodded along with my regular screening, and then in 2017 I started getting abscesses regularly between my front and back passages. I went to the GP a couple of times and was referred to a consultant. An MRI found nothing, but the abscesses kept recurring, so we repeated this a couple of times – off to the GP, referred to a consultant, sent for an MRI. The second time, something was found on the MRI – a problem with the lining of my womb. I didn't even know they would be able to see my womb on the MRI since they were investigating a problem elsewhere. This had nothing to do with the abscesses. I was referred to a gynaecologist who at first said everything seemed fine and not to worry but then changed his mind and ordered further tests when he heard about Lynch syndrome and CMMRD. By this time, it was early 2018. Around this time, I also had my annual gastroscopy. Then one week in May I was asked to come in to see Mr Rashed on the ward, not during his usual office hours, which was a bad sign. I had known the routine gastroscopy results probably weren't good because the gastroenterologist said he had found a flat polyp in my small intestine and sent it for urgent testing. Mr Rashed confirmed it was duodenal cancer. This is quite rare as the duodenum is the shortest section of the small intestine. I felt strangely calm because had almost been expecting it, but I didn't expect what happened next. The following day, I had an appointment at the gynaecology department, where I hoped we would discuss the abscesses I'd been having. Instead, the consultant told me the lining of my womb was definitely pre-cancerous and possibly cancerous. Two potential cancer diagnoses within two days. To say I was in a state of shock and fear feels like an understatement. After further testing a few weeks later, they confirmed the womb cancer was not pre-cancerous but in fact early-stage cancer. They were very surprised when I expressed relief because I had been worried that it would turn out to be a later stage somehow. Heck, whether it was pre-cancer or early-stage cancer something had to be done about it, so what difference did it make? At least it wasn't worse. There had to be something good to hold onto within that onslaught of bad news.

Since I had two cancers at once, there were different teams trying to decide what to do with me, and every consultant wanted me to be their patient. I was turning out to be quite popular and was greeted like a celebrity when I attended the second hospital I had been referred to. The plan was to deal with the uterine cancer first with a hysterectomy in September, then do a Whipple procedure in November for the duodenal cancer. My partner and I also saw a different consultant to discuss fertility options. We were told we could freeze my eggs for later use with a surrogate, but this process could stimulate the lining of the womb – in other words, the cancer – to grow further. We quickly decided my health was the most important thing and we didn't want to take any risks. So we said a sad goodbye to our chances of having biological children and went ahead with the plan. It was a total hysterectomy including removing my ovaries because ovarian cancer was also a potential risk with CMMRD. It was an open surgery and difficult to recover from, but still a walk in the park to recover from in comparison to the Whipple. Whipple surgery is often used to remove pancreatic cancer and involves taking out the head of the pancreas, the duodenum, the bile duct and the gall bladder. It was about an eight-hour surgery with two hours simply dealing with adhesions from my previous bowel surgery. Between the Whipple surgery and the hysterectomy, I was off work for five months. At the time of writing, I have had no cancer diagnoses since then. I am doing very well physically and mentally, although the burden of having regular tests to check for CMMRD-related cancers does take its toll.

This section has been a crash course in my cancer experiences, but if you would like to know more, I go into much more detail in my first memoir *Gut Feelings: Coping with Cancer and Living with Lynch Syndrome.*

The cancer experiences I have outlined above feel like they were all a very long time ago, but they have left their marks in various ways. Some are physical – the scars, the change in bowel habits, the hot flushes that come with surgical menopause. Some have changed my life plans, such as not being able to have children. Some are emotional changes – fear of recurrence, increased anxiety, the mental burden of planning appointments and changing schedules to fit things in. But dare I say it, some changes have been positive. I have a sense of urgency for doing the things I want to do right now, not "one day". I view growing old as a privilege and welcome birthdays as achievements instead of worrying about ageing. I have taken my cancer experiences and turned them into art – poetry, memoir, even a few drawings. I have used my experiences to connect with other people and to shape my career. It's been bad, but it's not all bad, and I've realised the importance of finding the good within the bad when living with a lifelong condition.

My Self In Brief

I am a Solitary Walk
Written on Friday 3rd December, 2021 at 16:23

I take my trainers for a walk
sneakers to my American friends
and they do sneak
pick up stones with their teeth
I am a solitary walk at lunch time
abandoning my desk
telling myself a twenty minute walk
is enough exercise
is better than nothing
and noting my thoughts as I walk
in a way I normally wouldn't
giving myself attention
for once
sneaking quality time
in the middle of the day

The order in which we talk about things when introducing ourselves is interesting. Do you start with relationships, jobs, hobbies, medical conditions? A lot of people don't want to lead with cancer, they want to lead with who else they are. For me, it's hard to know where to start when I talk about myself and am trying not to relate it to cancer. I think this is especially true when cancer occurs at a younger age – I was twenty-two and those are still formative years. I don't know what it's like to be an adult without a cancer experience or without that genetic risk hanging over my head. I don't know what it's like to feel like a normal healthy adult without medical concerns.

Something that I find myself doing these days is starting with where I am, not where I've been. I find when I'm thinking about cancer and CMMRD, I'm often writing more about where I am now, and less about what happened before – less about surgeries and more about what I'm thinking about now and what I'm worried about now – scans, appointments, what life is like living with this condition. I'm always keen to get people to understand – as much as they can understand – what life is like for me or for people like me. So sometimes I do lead with cancer, but I think it's also important in this book to give you a proper picture of myself because none of us are just our diagnoses.

I am thirty-five years old at the time of writing. My family is from Manchester but I was born in Northamptonshire. My partner and I still live here and from our bedroom window I can see the National Lift Tower in the distance, which I think of as the most inland lighthouse. I met my partner at university where we both did an I.T. degree. I have a few close friends. My parents, my sister, her husband and my niece and nephew live in the next town. I work for a charity, which I'll talk about later because it's an important part of the story. When I was first diagnosed with bowel cancer, I'd just finished university and I was looking for my first full-time job while working part-time at Sainsbury's. I had a couple of temporary jobs after that and then worked in digital marketing for ten years. In 2015 when I was working at a digital marketing agency, I decided I wanted to do a master's degree. I did my MA in Creative Writing while I was working. Then in 2019, I went part-time at work to begin my PhD and I'm still currently doing this. Sometimes I wonder what I would be doing in life, in my career, in my spare time if it wasn't for cancer. Would I still be doing my PhD? Would I still be working at my current job? Would I still have spent ten years in marketing or would I have done something else? These questions aren't particularly helpful because there's nothing you can do about them. You can't change the answers. There's no point regretting anything as you can't do anything about it. But it still makes me wonder.

While I don't work in digital marketing anymore, I still love the internet and computers and always have. I used to particularly enjoy making websites back in the early 2000s an am nostalgic for this time. Millennials remember dial-up internet, remember being told to get off the internet so that our parents could use the phone, using AOL Instant Messenger and MSN, burning songs onto CDs and before that, taping songs off the radio onto cassette. I used to hate listening to the radio because they didn't play any songs that I liked but now I like listening to BBC Radio 1. I love a wide range of music but especially early 2000s rock. I also like modern hip hop, and all the music my dad introduced me to when I was a kid, like Motown, and 60s, 70s and 80s rock. I love to sing but I'm terrible at it. If I could change one thing that would be completely inconsequential it would be to have a good singing voice.

A little more about me: my favourite colour is yellow. I like being weird and being passionate about my interests. I'm interested in Buddhism. I don't believe in fate – everything doesn't happen for a reason, things just happen and we make of them what we can. I like watching the same TV sitcoms over and over because it's comforting knowing what is going to happen. Perhaps my anxiety, particularly around health, impacts this.

Another thing that may be influenced by my health experiences is that I'm an all-or-nothing kind of thinker. This book is an example of this. I'm excited and impatient – I wanted to write this entire book in one weekend. I decided a while ago that I wanted to write a book about CMMRD but I didn't know exactly what it was going to be about or what angle it would take. I had already written my book on Lynch syndrome and I didn't want to simply retread old ground. I wanted to tell you something new and eventually, one Friday evening, I decided what I wanted that angle to be. It was quite obvious because it was something that I had been thinking about for a while. I started making notes in my notebook and then I went to bed. And while I was trying to get to sleep, the first few sentences of the book started coming into my head. So I wrote them down as I didn't want to forget them. And then I decided that I wanted to write the whole thing in one weekend. Between doing housework and having guests over, I managed to write a first draft by Sunday night. Once I get an idea in my head, I want to work on something until it's done – I want everything to happen right away. I think that is partially me and partially my cancer experiences.

I also like to travel and this is one way I inject excitement into my life amid the anxiety of hospital appointments. I love Florida, it's my favourite place. I also like my home comforts. I love food. I love anything that's not very good for me. I love being myself and not being concerned about what people think. I think I've not been very good at that lately but historically I have been and I'm trying. I'm a quiet person and sometimes people make me feel bad about that. It's difficult to feel good about it, to feel good about yourself, when people have been so critical of the natural way that you are, especially during childhood. Though I would be the first to say that I did have a wonderful childhood.

And then things got a bit more complicated.

Getting Genetic Testing

Awaiting
Written on Sunday 4th October, 2015 at 18:38

Awaiting acutely,
aching and awake –
far too awake, alert,
I wait
for days.
Artificial acrobatics, an
armful of blood
gone
anxiety escalated,
awaiting alleviation.
After the event,
agitation quietened,
quickly quelled, dispelled
until next time,
assessments and appointments,
awaiting a verdict again –
not-so-merry-go-round.

I first heard about Lynch syndrome long before I even stepped into the geneticist's office. This was thanks to a slight overstep from a doctor during one of my hospital stays. Looking at my chart and back up at my mother and me, he said "so I see you have Lynch syndrome". He was met with two very blank faces. We had never heard of Lynch syndrome and we said as much. The doctor hastily retreated and I can only guess that the clipboard said "suspected Lynch syndrome" or similar. But sure enough, he was basically correct.

My parents and I were referred to genetic testing after my bowel surgery, due to my age and how many polyps there were. We met our genetic counsellor, who told us that there could be several genetic reasons why I'd had bowel cancer. One was Familial Adenomatous Polyposis (FAP), which is another rare inherited condition (though it sometimes appears spontaneously). As the name suggests, it can cause lots of polyps to grow and can lead to bowel and other cancers. There was also another possibility mentioned to us that I can't remember, and out of the three of them, Lynch syndrome sounded the worst and I was very much hoping it wouldn't be that. My parents and I were sent appointments for blood tests so the genetic testing could be completed. We were called back to the genetics clinic some weeks later to find out the results. The geneticist explained that my parents had Lynch syndrome and that I had inherited it from both of them. She explained how genetic conditions are passed through the family and told us about the cancer risks involved. I am grateful to my geneticist because the way she explained it to me still helps me to explain it to other people today, and it has the potential for being a rather complex topic. No doubt at some point she said the word CMMRD, but I must not have taken it in because I simply identified as someone with Lynch syndrome for many years to come. At my appointment after the results were confirmed, my geneticist also asked me to undress and had a look at my skin. I thought at the time she was looking for skin cancer, but now I wonder if she was also looking for café-au-lait spots.

I didn't hear from my geneticist again for a few years once we had established my screening programme. It wasn't until after my surgeries in 2018 that she called me and I filled her in on my two cancer diagnoses, which she had not been aware of. She was actually calling to ask me if I would like to have a regular brain MRI and a full-body MRI. What an offer! My first instinct was "God, no", but I agreed to hear more about it so she sent me an appointment to come and see her in person. It was some time after the COVID lockdowns when I eventually got there.

What followed was something I initially thought of as an amusing negotiation as if for a used car, but I now recognise as important shared decision making. Did I want to have a brain MRI? No – my brother died from a brain tumour and I was terrified that was going to happen to me. I didn't want to be faced with this idea on a regular basis. My geneticist said that CMMRD screening guidelines recommended having a brain MRI every six months, as well as a full body MRI every year. So far, the screening I was already undergoing was traumatic enough. I had a CT scan every year for five years after my surgery, a yearly gastroscopy, a flexible sigmoidoscopy every two years, and since my Whipple procedure, a capsule endoscopy every year.

I'll pause here to give you a quick breakdown of what those last three procedures are if you are unfamiliar with them:

A gastroscopy is when a camera is put down the throat to look inside the food pipe, stomach, and the first part of the small intestine. They use a throat spray to numb your throat, and I always ask for sedation as well because it is my least favourite procedure due to the gagging and discomfort.

A flexible sigmoidoscopy is similar to a colonoscopy but it doesn't go as far or take as long. Since I don't have a bowel, I can't have a colonoscopy anymore so the flexible sigmoidoscopy, or flexi sig for short, looks at my internal pouch instead.

A capsule endoscopy is when you go to the hospital and swallow a camera inside a capsule the size of a large vitamin pill. The capsule passes through your system, taking lots of images as it goes. You wear recording equipment around your waist for the day, which captures the images. With this test, you can go about your daily business as normal while it's recording. After a few hours, the camera passes with your poo and you can take off the recording equipment and return it to the hospital. This test can take photos of the entire area it passes through, giving the doctor more information than they may get from other endoscopies. There is a difference in this procedure for me because I have had Whipple surgery and since then, the camera no longer passes through my system and sometimes spins in place for hours instead. This means I have to have my capsule placed via gastroscopy, so I have both procedures done at the same time.

So did I want to add another appointment into that equation? Not really. I "negotiated" my geneticist down from six-monthly brain MRIs to yearly, and agreed to the yearly full body scan as well. These now take place at the same time, meaning I spend at least an hour in the MRI machine. As much as I didn't want to think about cancer or for anxiety (or "scanxiety") to interfere with my life more than it already did, I understood the importance of screening, especially with my increased cancer risk. In November 2022 when I was referred to a consultant at St Mark's Hospital who specialised in Lynch syndrome, I would also negotiate with him to increase my two-yearly sigmoidoscopies to one per year instead of one every six months. I simply didn't want to spend half my life going to or worrying about appointments or the results of scans. I knew I was stuck with this condition and these tests for my whole life, so I wanted to do it all on my own terms and in a way I thought I could handle. I should point out here that after binge-watching The Good Doctor, which features many patients with brain tumours, in 2023 I contacted my geneticist and asked to change to the recommended six-monthly brain scans. There is a balance to strike between doing what is recommended and doing what you can handle, and we don't always get there immediately. I am not perfect at doing everything recommended to me, but I am getting there and I say yes to most things.

Here is a list of my current scans, which may not be exactly the same as other people's but gives you an idea of what has been offered to me and what I am doing:

Screening	Frequency Offered	Frequency Agreed
Brain MRI	Six months	Yearly initially, then six months
Full body MRI	Yearly	Yearly (same time as one of the six-monthly brain MRIs)
Capsule endoscopy	Yearly	Yearly (same time as gastroscopy)
Gastroscopy	Yearly	Yearly
Flexible sigmoidoscopy	Six-months (increased from every two years in 2023)	Yearly
Blood test for leukaemia	Six months	Six months
CT scan	Post-surgery only (yearly for five years)	Yearly for five years
Abdominal ultrasound	Six months	Declined, as the benefit sounded uncertain if already having a full-body MRI

To put it into real terms, here is what the last year or so has looked like for me:

Date	Screening
August 2022	Gastroscopy with capsule endoscopy
September 2022	Flexible sigmoidoscopy
December 2022	CT scan
March 2023	Brain MRI and full body MRI
March 2023	Repeat gastroscopy with capsule endoscopy (last capsule endoscopy images were not clear enough)
August 2023	Blood test for leukaemia
September 2023	Brain MRI

As you can see from the second entry for March 2023, not only are these tests carried out regularly, but sometimes they are completed even more frequently if they need to be redone. In this instance, the bowel prep I took wasn't clear enough for the camera to get a good picture, so we had to do it again. This was through no fault of my own as I followed the preparation to the letter – sometimes these things just happen and it's very frustrating.

There has also previously been mention of a urine test, for which a letter was sent to my GP but nothing has yet come of that. At the time of writing, my geneticist is going by recommendations from the US and awaiting European guidelines, which may prompt us to do something different.

My geneticist also recommended I take aspirin every day, which may reduce bowel cancer risk in people with Lynch syndrome,[8] and therefore could also work in people with CMMRD. I am prescribed 300mg per day but the dose prescribed varies from person to person.

During the appointment with my geneticist, which must have been around 2021, I realised that the proper name for my "double Lynch syndrome" was CMMRD. I don't know why that had not filtered through in our first appointments together years ago. Too much information, perhaps – too many new words. I had always simply said I had Lynch syndrome, but it may have been at this point that I realised there was a completely different term for what I had. However, I still didn't want to think about my increased cancer risk. It was scary enough thinking about the increased risk associated with Lynch syndrome, let alone an even bigger risk on top of that.

---

[8] 'New Draft Guidance Says Aspirin Taken Daily Could Reduce Risk of Bowel Cancer for People with Lynch Syndrome', Bowel Cancer UK, https://www.bowelcanceruk.org.uk/news-and-blogs/news/new-draft-guidance-says-aspirin-taken-daily-could-reduce-risk-of-bowel-cancer-for-people-with-lynch-syndrome/.

What is Acceptance?

I'd like to share some of my journal writing here to show some of my early thinking about whether or not I had achieved acceptance:

Accepting Cancer
Written on Saturday 1ˢᵗ August, 2020

I have been thinking about acceptance – what is it really, and do I even have any experience in it? I guess I always assumed I had accepted cancer and everything that came with it. But did I? I am wondering if I ever really accepted how cancer has changed my life. The added stresses, appointments and so on. I feel like I haven't accepted that appointments would crop up regularly and that I would need to work around them. I mean, in a practical sense I do that anyway, and I know they are coming and that I will need to make arrangements. But have I accepted it on an emotional level, that this is how things will be forever now? Have I made peace with it? Almost certainly not.

And each appointment is a new thing to have to make peace with. I wonder if there is a way to make peace with the situation as a whole, which means anything that occurs is automatically accepted as default. Like organising incoming emails into an "accepted" folder. I guess the problem with that is you can let in a lot of rubbish that way – spam, trolling, negativity, jobs you don't want to do. I mean, you don't have to accept everything. Some things you might want to change, and if you can change them, there's no point in accepting them if you're not happy to. That's a lack of control, and that's another problem. You don't have to accept everything. But if you have no other choice, you might as well.

Knowledge vs. Acceptance

As the above paragraph I journalled in 2020 explains, I had assumed I had accepted cancer and Lynch syndrome, and it wasn't until I interrogated my innermost workings a little deeper that I realised I hadn't really accepted it at all. I was getting knowledge confused with acceptance, and knowing something is going to happen and accepting it are two different things. Even if you acknowledge that something is happening, and agree to deal with it and make accommodations so that it can happen, that isn't necessarily acceptance. And I needed acceptance because it was so difficult to be pulled from normal daily life into the medical world every time a new appointment or set of results cropped up.

Moving Between Two Worlds

What I hit on in the journal entry was that I was treating each appointment, surgery, screening, and cancer diagnosis as an individual event rather than part of a whole – the whole of course being CMMRD, though I didn't think about it in those exact terms at the time. I wondered if it would help for me to accept that I was a person with CMMRD, that CMMRD was an ongoing thing that was always there, rather than something that came and went like a horrible tide pulling scalpels and hospital gowns to my shores when I least expected it. I often felt as if I were straddling two worlds, trying to

43

exist in the "normal" world while the medical world was waiting for me and could pounce at any moment. I would be in the office at the digital marketing agency where I worked at the time and I would get a phone call from the hospital asking to book me in for an appointment. All of a sudden I'm not thinking about writing blog posts or emailing my clients; I'm once again considering the prospect of the cancer returning and having to ask my boss for time off to go to my screening. But what if I didn't have to deal with it all bit by bit? After all, you don't need to worry about returning to the medical world if you never leave it. Is that really better? At first, I thought it was admitting defeat to resign myself to the reality that I would always be going back and forth to the hospital. But acceptance is not defeat. It could in fact mean more peace of mind.

This idea of balancing two worlds is something I would also consider later as I worked on my PhD. In 2019, when I was recovering from surgery by filling my life with everything but the kitchen sink, I applied to start my PhD in October. I was – and at the time of writing still am – researching my own cancer experiences through writing poetry and prose. I'm investigating how writing helps me shape meaning from my cancer experiences. What started out as writing solely about cancer soon morphed into something more, as I realised I didn't just want to write about cancer. I have always been a writer, though I didn't start writing about cancer until two years after my initial diagnosis, in 2012. A little way into my PhD, I realised that I hadn't stopped writing about cancer since 2012 and actually, I wanted to write about other things. In fact, writing about other things could even benefit me as much as writing about cancer did. After three diagnoses and amidst constant screening, I was feeling very much like a cancer patient and not much else. Who else was I apart from someone who had had cancer? Where was the rest of my identity? I wanted to write about that, and in writing about other parts of myself and finding myself, I hoped to find a place where cancer could slot in a little more neatly and consistently as a smaller presence, rather than taking over entirely several times per year. This is reflected in my writing, as I tend to categorise my poems as either cancer-related or non-cancer. Imagine that – there is cancer, and then there is everything else grouped together. My identity, my relationships, my interests, and anything else I might think to write about – in fact, anything else that exists. It's as if cancer is of the same size and magnitude as everything else in the world combined! For me, acceptance helps me to recognise this and work towards making this representation of cancer a little smaller in my mind and in my life, while still being at peace with its presence. And the reverse is also true – being able to make cancer that little bit smaller helps with acceptance.

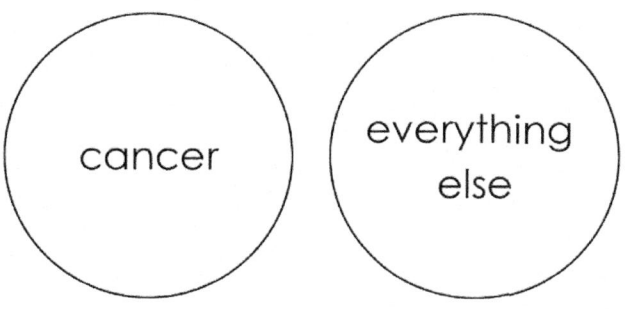

I have now come to the conclusion that it helps to think of myself as someone with a genetic condition rather than solely a cancer survivor because that at least goes some way towards explaining or acknowledging the ongoing surveillance and the stress that comes with that. Part of the benefit of accepting it and looking at it as one long-term condition rather than lots of different cancers is the impact it has had on my willingness to go to screening. I would not have changed my mind about the frequency of my brain MRIs if I had not been in that place of acceptance.

Moving Towards Acceptance

But how do we get to acceptance? How did I get to acceptance? It's a difficult question to answer and I think there are a few factors – time, attitude, and maybe even exposure. Some definitions explain acceptance as not resisting something. My first thought on this was that I've never actively resisted – I've never skipped out on appointments or screening. I suppose I have avoided thinking about CMMRD, which is a kind of resistance. So perhaps it's helpful to think about the ways in which we resist or avoid the subject, whether that is by physically not doing something or going somewhere, or mentally not allowing ourselves to think about or talk about the situation. Once we know the ways our lack of acceptance appears, we can work towards addressing them. Why do we do this? How does it make us feel? What can we do instead? How would that work and how would it help? If only it were as easy as clicking on "Accept all" on a website's cookie banner.

I used to have moments of disbelief: *I can't believe this is me, I can't believe all this happened.* Now I've gone from "how has this happened?" to "this has happened." And it's still happening, so being able to accept that is incredibly helpful. Because nothing will stop me from having CMMRD. It will always be there. For example, my partner and I often dream of winning the lottery. We talk about the holidays we would go on, how we'd quit our jobs and where we'd live. But all the money in the world and all the joy and nice things and love won't stop me from having CMMRD.

This is taken from my blog and was written on 12th June 2022 – another small step towards acceptance:

I could finish my PhD
I can feel fulfilled by my career
I could get married and we could adopt a kid
We could get two pet cats
I could live to be 40, 50, 60, 70, even 80
But I will never stop having CMMRD

We could win the lottery and that wouldn't change my yearly tests – not the fact I have to have them or the outcome of them.

I could have all the good fortune and success in the world and that won't reduce my cancer risk, it won't alleviate my anxiety, it won't change my health.

And I guess on the surface, this comes from a place of despair, of knowing my health worries won't end until I die. And that might make everything seem a bit pointless.

But beyond that, on the flip side, there is acceptance.

If I can accept this state of affairs,
if I can realise what won't change and take solace in
what will,
if I can come to terms with my condition and what's
required to keep me alive and well,
if I can take this as part and parcel of my life –

maybe fulfilment and success are possible, and maybe
peace of mind is that little bit more attainable.

From Denial To Definition

body ode
Written on Sunday 23rd April, 2017 at 11:34

reasons why my body is awesome:

low blood pressure
very little trouble sleeping
haven't vomited since January 2011
bones all intact

badass scars
cute dimple at old stoma site
super-efficient waste disposal system
totally flat lower stomach
tattoos

clear skin
soles of feet have a pleasing arch
mad hair that sometimes looks pretty good
ambiguously-coloured eyes
back curves in, bottom sticks out
boobs
pretty good legs
GREAT hands
ticklish
baby face needs ID for buying alcohol
can smell onion rings cooking at twenty paces

There may be some people who counter the points I made in the previous chapter. People who say "don't let cancer define you". "Don't be defined by your illness." But I don't think it's as simple as that, and I don't find those statements very helpful. It makes it sound like I have more control than I really do. It makes me feel like I am "doing" cancer survivorship wrong somehow, or that other people would do things differently. It makes me feel like I need to try harder, like I'm wallowing too much and should be over it, or worst of all like there is something wrong with my identity. As I mentioned, my identity has become a large part of my exploration of my cancer and CMMRD experiences, and it's a complicated topic. If I have swung wildly from complete ignorance and denial to defining myself by the very thing I was avoiding, is that okay or not? Is there a happy medium somewhere in between? Am I really doing it all wrong?

These are questions I have asked myself many times, and I may not be the only one. But the first thing to address is that nobody is doing survivorship wrong. We're all out here doing the best we can, and if that means only thinking about our conditions when we absolutely have to, that's fine. If it means scaling a mountain to raise money for charity and increase awareness of a disease, that's fine too. And if like me you've cemented CMMRD, Lynch syndrome or cancer into your life, then you keep doing you. In this section, I will attempt to explain how I got to this point, and I think it would help to show you a timeline of what has happened so far:

Timeline

2010	January	A&E visit
	June	Bowel cancer diagnosed
	July	Bowel removed, stoma created
2011	January	Stoma reversed and internal pouch created
	September	Genetic testing confirmed CMMRD
2012		First started writing about cancer and published a prose piece
2013		Sadness and fear
2014		Published first article about cancer experiences
2015		More sadness and fear
2016		Slowly absorbing Lynch syndrome into my life and understanding it
2017	October	Tried counselling for the first time
2018	May	Uterine cancer and duodenal cancer diagnoses
	September	Hysterectomy
	November	Whipple surgery
2019	January	Started writing memoir
	October	Started PhD
2020		Continued PhD, writing about cancer, Lynch syndrome and identity beyond illness
2021	February	Published Lynch syndrome memoir
	January	Made first podcast appearances
2022	January	Started to accept CMMRD
2023	January	Started working for a bowel cancer and bowel disease charity
	July	Wrote this book

2010, 2011 and 2012

I will skip over 2010 and 2011 because I have already gone through this period when talking about my cancer stories in an earlier chapter. What I will say is that when I was going through the diagnosis, testing and surgeries, and then learning how to live with a stoma, it was very much a case of taking things one day at a time and dealing with whatever I needed to in the moment. It wasn't until things settled down – probably in 2012 after my genetic testing – that I began to feel so very sad about everything that had happened, and scared about what could be yet to come. Many people I have spoken to said they experienced the same – that the emotional effects of their cancer experiences hit them after the event, once they were able to process everything that had happened. This is something that seems to often surprise people, and I certainly wasn't expecting it.

I was also very much in denial right from the beginning because when I was diagnosed I remember saying I didn't have cancer, but I think that was partly because of the way I was told about my diagnosis. Mr Rashed said they had found many polyps and some of them had cells that were cancerous. My brain simply didn't connect "some of the cells are cancerous" to thinking "I have cancer". Or maybe it didn't want to. Perhaps it's because people always think it won't happen to them; maybe that's true even after you've heard it. Regardless, it's more evidence that I was in quite a bit of denial right from the beginning.

However, in 2012 I started writing about cancer and had my first cancer-related prose piece published in an online literary journal. It was called "2010" and was about a page long, and in it, I describe sitting in my bed in 2012 while experiencing intrusive memories of going into surgery. At this point, I was still very much dealing with previous cancer experiences and worrying about it coming back, rather than thinking about Lynch syndrome or CMMRD.

2013 – 2016

I'd like to present this poem, or assortment of poem-adjacent thoughts, from around 2015 and later to help illustrate my state of mind around this time:

Conversations With Myself, Several Years Cancer-Free
Circa 2015

falling so deep into scared you forget what triggered it
so far inside my own head I'm not sure how I got here
I can only apologise to myself.

I am sorry.

I don't know how I don't know how I don't know how I
don't know how I don't

the darkplace is too difficult to describe and I've lost my
way too deep inside to find the way out

It takes too much effort and I'm scared to try
but it's all in my head it's all in my head it's all in my
head it's all in my

Why does this keep happening? I don't know I don't know.

There is more to life than this
and I know what it is I just
don't know where I put it.

every so often my nervousness is reset
fear heightened for only nine hours of the day – 9am-
6pm is when they can call
or when post can arrive
between that it's low grade worry only

Imagine having a cancer scare once a year, or more
than once a year. that's what going for checkups is.
That's what scanxiety is. That's what being a survivor
is, especially a survivor with a genetic condition.

I try to prepare myself for the worst so another
diagnosis doesn't sneak up on me.
Does it really hurt more if you're less prepared for it?
Yes, I have discovered. Yes.
But the more I am given, the more I can handle.

It's never actually over. That's the problem. Constant
fight or flight. Constant edge of seat.

I spoke to someone eventually. Paid a professional.
Then found out it's hard feeling anxious and tormented
but being told you don't actually have a mental health
problem.

Imagine people are having a normal conversation with
you and you're normal on the outside but on the inside
you're shouting I can't be normal like this when I don't
feel like it, it's too much hard work.

darkplace.
that place is close
and it is easy
to return to

PTSD:

Panic
Tension
Shame
Distress

Petrifying
Trauma
Self
Diagnosis

Please don't tell me this is just for soldiers returning
from the war. Don't belittle everything I've seen.

There is more than one definition of war.

Why do you think people use those terrible cancer as a
war/fight analogies? I don't like them but maybe for the
purposes of illustrating what trauma is, they may be
worth something.

Oh hello again, flashbacks

oh hell again
I thought we were done here, but
obviously not.

An aspirin a day
might *keep those shadows away.*

I think I prefer the feeling of distress to the
mundaneness of uncertainty
and I prefer the sadness of looking back - the wallowing
- to the worrying about what might happen.

I feel like shaking myself –
what are you doing to yourself
and why?

I don't know.

"You need to stop."
"I don't know how."
Tell me how.

My Friday nights around 2015 often consisted of drinking Jack Daniels, listening to music and writing rather bleak poetry that frankly probably wasn't fit for public consumption. But at least I was writing and that was providing an outlet. In fact, I published my first article about my cancer experiences on Cancer.net and that was the beginning of submitting my patient stories to health and charity websites. I wrote my first article about Lynch syndrome for a fellow Lynchie's blog in 2015. I would spend the next seven years or so writing and talking about Lynch syndrome when as we know, my diagnosis was a little different. I do regret that to an extent, but as may become apparent, it's been part of a process and maybe that was necessary to get to where I am today.

2017 and 2018

After years of feeling sad about everything that had happened to me, not to mention worrying about the future and dealing with the associated bad dreams and intrusive memories, I had been starting to wonder if I should talk to someone about it. I didn't want to go through the NHS to find a counsellor because I didn't want it to be another thing I had to go through the system for and I wanted control over this part of my experience. So I chose a counsellor and saw her for six sessions. I wasn't sure how helpful it really was, though I would revisit counselling with other people later on. Not long after I stopped seeing her, I received my two new cancer diagnoses in 2018, and you know what happened during the rest of that year.

2019 and 2020

The work I have been doing for my PhD has greatly helped me to deal with cancer-related issues. Not only have I been writing about cancer, but about my childhood, my feelings around being quiet or introverted, and the things I love like music, Christmas and holidays.

In 2019, I started writing my memoir, but it wasn't until 2021 that I finally released it. In fact, the book I originally set out to write was going to be a self-help book for people diagnosed with Lynch syndrome. What was it, how was it diagnosed, what did it mean, what screening was involved and how could people cope emotionally? The problem was, I couldn't cope emotionally with writing the thing. I didn't want to research the percentages of cancer risks involved with Lynch syndrome. I didn't want to know all the different cancers and which gene mutations they were related to. I didn't want to see questions about life expectancies popping up in Google's "People also asked" section while I was looking for other things. I couldn't bear to wade through the science, even for the sake of writing and publishing a book, helping other people and feeling the sense of accomplishment that would provide. It wasn't going to happen.

Instead, I decided to write my memoir. I wrote a little at a time, about everything that had happened to me from 2010 to early 2019. And then I smashed out a first draft over just a few days. I returned to it and edited it when I could over the years, but it hurt to revisit events. It made me sad all over again. And still, this was me talking about cancer experiences and Lynch syndrome – not CMMRD.

2021

In 2021, after trying and failing to get my memoir published, I decided I would do it myself. I edited it to a standard I was happy with, created a cover, and put it on Amazon. I didn't want to be forced by an editor to keep revisiting this painful material. I wanted to do everything on my terms and as long as I was happy with it, that was all that mattered. I released the book in February 2021 and hosted a book launch online where I read from the book and took questions from my modest but enthusiastic audience. Alongside this, I was doing some marketing and outreach by way of writing guest blog posts. Also in 2021, though somewhat unrelated to the book release, I made my first appearances as a guest on various podcasts. Still, I was only talking about Lynch syndrome. It wasn't until 2022 that I reached my ultimate turning point and finally began to think about and accept CMMRD.

My Turning Point

CMMRD stands for Constitutional Mismatch Repair Deficiency and...

Written on Sunday 6ᵗʰ March, 2022 at 11:56

Confidently Managing My Rare Disease
Cheese Makes Meals Really Delicious
Creating Mayhem, Madness and Random Distractions
Calm, Mild Mannered and Rational Daughter
Chicken Makes My Rice Dish
Constantly Making a Mess Relishing Dessert
Campaign for More Music, Rhythm and Dancing
Communicating Medical Metaphor Research and
Development
Chief Manager of Major Rhyming Decisions
Centre for Mysterious Magic and Ridiculous Dares
Central Manifesto for More Revealing Dresses
Comfortable Mattress Morning Relaxation
Demonstration
Counting Many Millions of RainDrops

I have a man called Dave to thank for my CMMRD turning point, though he may not have realised it at the time. Dave Dubin runs a Lynch syndrome website and podcast called Alive and Kick'n and I was a guest on the podcast in early 2022. For starters, it was refreshing talking to someone about my experiences without first having to explain what Lynch syndrome is – his whole organisation and podcast is about that, and as someone with Lynch syndrome himself, he knew all about it. Because most people who appear on the podcast have Lynch syndrome, it made sense to try to find a unique angle, and having CMMRD provided that. Listening back to the episode now, I wasn't even sure of the name of CMMRD! But I was heartened to find that Dave had heard of it, and I had the opportunity to tell him the story of my experiences so far. After we had finished speaking, I was left feeling like I still wanted to talk about CMMRD. So I did. I went onto an app called Wisdom that I had started using. It is an audio app where people create talks and listeners can tune in live or later on. So I hopped onto Wisdom and explained about the podcast that I had been on and explored my feelings around CMMRD a little bit more. Dave had helped me to prise open those floodgates.

The experience of talking on a podcast has always been an enjoyable one for me, particularly as a guest rather than a host. With Dave and many others, it was easy for me to open up and talk about my experiences. It reminded me that I wasn't alone and that people were interested and wanted to understand. It also gave me a way to express myself differently – talking about something can sometimes bring up ideas that I might not have thought of if I were writing, and the podcast presenter always plays a big part in that. Talking about CMMRD with Dave was particularly beneficial because I always wondered what community I fitted into. I always felt slightly different to people in other medical communities because I had a stoma for different reasons to them, or because I had Lynch syndrome in the family and they didn't. Or because I had pain I wanted to ask about but I didn't know which community to ask because I didn't know which surgery had caused it. Having the opportunity to talk about CMMRD helped me realise that was where I fitted in. It encompasses all of my experiences rather than just one. Identifying with CMMRD was beginning to make the most sense, and there would be benefits once I could accept this part of my story.

Raring To Go

hope water egg sauce
Written on Wednesday 13ᵗʰ April, 2022 at 22:16

hope seeps in like water
the smallest amount can get through the tiniest crack
like field mice wiggling into my living room
through holes I cannot find

hope seeps in like water
except it's bright, glowing
like yolk
because hope is a bit like water which
is a bit like runny egg
and runny egg is basically sauce

see it ooze in under the door
smear it on toast
lick it off your fingers
feed it to the mice

let in a tiny bit and then —

the floodgates open

Talking to Dave and speaking on Wisdom were small events that started the gradual seeping in of my acceptance of CMMRD. I gradually let myself think about the condition and what it meant. These were things I already knew, but I had spent a long time identifying as someone with only Lynch syndrome, despite that not being my exact diagnosis. I considered, and still consider, myself to be part of the Lynch syndrome community, which has been very helpful and welcoming to me. At some point, I looked for similar communities for CMMRD. I joined a Facebook group and found some people to follow on Twitter who were talking about it. There aren't many of us, but there are people who understand. Finding those people has helped me to accept it more. And I should say that none of this is deliberate. I didn't set out to talk about CMMRD, to research it, or to accept it. It is something that happened naturally over time, which is why it is difficult to advise someone else on how to do it. Sometimes things happen when they are ready to happen. There's a time and a place for everything.

Take my day job as a prime example. In March 2022, the digital marketing agency I worked for took on a new client, the charity Bowel Research UK. As someone who had experienced bowel cancer, I was keen to work with this client, and they also asked me to do some freelance guest blogging for them, talking about my experiences as a patient. Naturally, this included talking about Lynch syndrome. After about seven months of working together, the CEO of the charity contacted me to let me know of a job opening as Patient and Public Involvement Manager at the charity. By this time I was in year four of my PhD and wondering what my next career move would be. I didn't want to have a doctorate in creative writing and cancer survivorship and be working in a field entirely unrelated to that. So I had already been weighing up my options between nonprofit, industry, or an academic career. This job aligned perfectly with my PhD and personal interests, so I agreed to an interview and happily accepted when the job was offered to me.

Had that job been available just a few years previously, I would have been in no fit state to take it. Years after my bowel cancer surgery I was still reeling over that first diagnosis, as well as my genetic condition. Then in 2018, I had my next two cancers. After those, I didn't feel as blindsided as I did the first time, and the emotional effects didn't hit me as hard as I thought they would. However, I still wasn't in a place of complete acceptance. I think what has helped has been writing about my experiences and doing this in a positive and purposeful way through my PhD research and writing my memoir. Writing my memoir really helped me to make sense of everything that happened by laying it all out chronologically and getting my thoughts in order. Then, working on my PhD gave me additional purpose and made me imagine my readers – both the people who haven't had cancer who I wanted to help understand those experiences, and also those who did have cancer who I wanted to give a feeling of empathy, understanding and belonging. Having those people in mind – and having great reactions from people who read my memoir – really helped me find my place in the world. This in turn helped me to be ready for my career change.

Add to that, the job itself has also helped me, and I say this when I'm only about six months in. A few years ago I couldn't bear to read about cancer research, other people's experiences, or the scientific side of things because it all felt too close to home. I did read some personal stories, but it got too real quite quickly. The difference now is that I'm in a better place, and I feel able to read both personal and professional literature. The more scientific research I read about, the more it helps me because it gives me the experience of being exposed to the subject of cancer without being too close to it. They aren't personal stories, and they're often not things that have happened to me or that I am currently worrying about happening to me. They help me to be present in the bowel cancer environment without being too close to it or feeling triggered by it. I suppose it could be considered a kind of exposure therapy. It has certainly helped me to write this book, which is something else I could not have faced doing just a couple of years ago. It feels natural now.

A surreal moment came when I attended a conference for the Association of Coloproctologists of Great Britain and Ireland (ACPGBI) in July 2023. Bowel Research UK had a stand there and I was in attendance for the whole three days of networking – a great achievement for someone with social anxiety. I was standing in the exhibition hall talking to a woman at one of the stands about the colonic irrigation product her company manufactured. And as we both stood there leaning over this model bowel, her pointing with one hand and holding the enema-like kit in the other as she explained how it worked, I found myself feeling amused, perplexed and strangely comfortable. How on earth had I ended up in this place, talking to this person about bowels as if it were the most normal thing in the world?

But it was. I had found my people. This was further affirmed when I was "spotted" during the conference by three different people who recognised me from my activity in the online cancer and Lynch syndrome community. I have spent a lot of time over the years on Twitter talking about my cancer experiences, my PhD research and my book. The cancer community on social media is huge and talking with my fellow "Lynchies" seemed to have been getting me noticed. Not only was I a PhD researcher, working for a medical charity, and a one-in-a-million CMMRD rarity... I was a little bit famous.

There is No Right or Wrong in CMMRD

superheroes
Written on Tuesday 26th December, 2017 at 11:25

superheroes don't wear capes - they
wear pyjamas or hospital gowns,
sometimes frowns more than smiles.
heroines are made from being
partially naked in front of strangers
who poke and prod and murmur and nod.
champions are diagnosed and delegated
these roles and in the end still may say
"I am not strong".

Dealing with Stress

That's been my story so far, but you don't need to do any of this. You don't have to do a PhD, work for a charity, or be an online CMMRD advocate. You don't need to talk about CMMRD to strangers, climb some mountain to raise thousands of pounds, or sell your story to the press. If you want to do any of those things, that's great – you do you. But if you just want to exist, if you just want to help your child with CMMRD, if you just want to get through your next scan, if you just want to hide under the covers while you're waiting for your results, those are all valid. Heck, who doesn't spend the odd day wrapped in a blanket on the couch and hiding from the world? Sometimes it's difficult to know what to do for the best. Sometimes we might want to advocate for ourselves and other people, and sometimes there might only be one human in the world we want to bother talking to. We're all just trying to get by and doing our best for ourselves and our families. Because make no mistake about it, the CMMRD life is hard. Here are a couple of passages from my memoir *Gut Feelings: Coping with Cancer and Living with Lynch Syndrome* to illustrate this point:

I hate the anxiety of receiving a letter that's clearly from the hospital. Post apocalypse, you might call it. The appointment might not be for a month or so, and once I've booked the time off work, I'll put it out of my mind quite easily for a couple of weeks. It's a bit of a honeymoon period. Then the appointment will get closer. I'll start to think about it more. I don't want to go. I hate hospitals. I hate having to go to these things. What are they going to find? Will it all be okay? The procedure is

73

so uncomfortable. What if they find something and I have to go through more tests, more surgery, or the scary unknowns – chemo, radiotherapy? The anxiety gets worse the closer it gets to the appointment. I'll forget about it during the day because I'll be distracted by something else, but then I'll remember and my stomach will lurch.

The anxiety isn't over when the test is done though, of course. With the gastroscopy and flexi sig, if everything is okay I usually find out there and then. If a sample needs to be sent away for a biopsy test, however, or if I've had a CT scan, I need to wait for the results to come back. Which again, can be sort of forgotten about for the first few days. I don't expect to hear back straight away, so I put it to the back of my mind for a while. But when two weeks have passed and there's still no letter, and I call the consultant's secretary or my GP office to try to chase up the results, that's when the anxiety kicks in again. Why is it taking so long? When will the results come? What will they say?

It's better to go through "scanxiety" than not go at all. And I say this as someone who earlier today thought "My CT scan was a couple of weeks ago so I should be getting a letter soon... unless I don't get a letter. What if they call me instead and say they need to make an appointment with my consultant to discuss the results because something isn't right? Because it's come back?" And my stomach falls through the floor. But I put it out of my mind, think of something else – until next time, at least. The fear is still better than the alternative.

Add to this, right now I am waiting for results from a capsule endoscopy but I am putting off chasing the hospital because I don't want to open that can of worms. As it's been months and I haven't heard anything, chances are it's fine and the hospital is doing some kind of "no-news-is-good-news" thing. Either way, doing all of the admin and advocacy often required of patients can take a lot of mental energy, and with plenty of other things in everyday life to manage, sometimes I just can't face the stress.

One thing to add here is that it may be that having a diagnosis of CMMRD may go some way to providing a little understanding of why cancer happened. My parents have explained to me that when my brother had a brain tumour, they wondered why it had happened. Could it have been the radiation from the Chernobyl disaster in 1986? Was it caused by the local distribution electrical substation on our street? It would be around twenty-five years before we discovered the real reason why it happened, but at least now there is an answer.

Choosing What We Think About and How

And stress isn't the only thing to face. What about death? Having had three different types of cancer and living with a rare condition, it's hardly surprising that I've thought about what happens when I die. I often think that I'll probably get a brain tumour and die young because it's kind of amazing I've gotten this far. I hope I've had all the cancers I will get but I just don't know. So it has crossed my mind, in the middle of the night or even as a rude interruption to my regular day, that at some point my partner and I will get the worst news and I'll have to leave him, and both of us having to deal with that is the worst part of it all. On a somewhat lighter note, I have my funeral all picked out. I know what song I want to be played, where I want to be buried. I'd like an eco-burial and a memorial cherry tree. I've put it all in my will and it sounds lovely. Yes, I enjoyed researching all of this. Perhaps it's the sense of control. I think I am more afraid of suffering in life than actually being dead. I don't think I could truly say for sure until I have to face it, but generally, I think I prioritise quality of life over quantity. I'd take less time if it would be more comfortable.

Something that helps me deal with CMMRD is having control over how I think about it. I used to think about my cancer experiences as three different incidents, but now that I'm coming to terms with CMMRD (which may still be a work in progress), I'm realising that it's one long condition that is always there, and that helps in some ways. As I said before, you can't be pulled back into the medical world if you never leave it. However, although it's a lifelong and life-limiting condition, CMMRD is not a disability. The Equality Act 2010 defines disability as "if you have a physical or mental impairment that has a 'substantial' and 'long-term' negative effect on your ability to do normal daily activities.[9] I always ponder over this question when filling out forms. Do you have a disability? Well no, but... Do you have a condition that affects your everyday life

---

[9] 'Definition of Disability under the Equality Act 2010 - GOV.UK', https://www.gov.uk/definition-of-disability-under-equality-act-2010.

or your ability to carry out tasks? Well no, but... it's not that simple. Thinking of it in those terms feels invalidating. It might not be a condition that impairs my daily function, but it's real and it has the potential for huge consequences. In this way, it matters how we characterise our conditions. I wouldn't want to say I have a disability when I don't, but I also wouldn't want my experiences to be downplayed when I do have this lifelong condition that has already resulted in three cancer diagnoses, three major operations, a total of over eight months when I was unable to work, several tests and scans every single year, infertility, and a level of fear and anxiety that I otherwise wouldn't have experienced. It's not a disability but all of that cannot be ignored. That's why I find it helpful to remember it's a lifelong condition that I have to deal with and when I'm finding that difficult, I should give myself a little grace.

I also find it helpful to challenge how I think about individual appointments. For example, I try to think of appointment letters as invitations and remember that I have control over whether I attend. The fact that I do always attend means I'm choosing to take care of myself.

Being Changed by CMMRD

If CMMRD has changed anything about a person, that is also fine and let's face it, not surprising. For example, I have always had a sense of urgency but my cancer experiences and facing my mortality have increased that. As I explained earlier, this book is an example of this. I work quickly once an idea grabs me. I can be impatient and sometimes impulsive and I want everything to be done already. That's partly me and probably partly my condition. I'm okay with it.

As I mentioned before, I appreciate birthdays more. I think growing old is a privilege and I hope I get to experience it. Cancer and genetic conditions change your perspective on life and it isn't always bad. I sometimes wonder about arrested development, too. Having cancer at the age of 22 means I haven't had a normal adulthood and sometimes I still feel like a child. Being a patient and losing some of your control might contribute to that.

It is really hard living with increased cancer risk and all of the scans, appointments and fears that come with it. We deal with things when we can – again, there's no right or wrong when trying to deal with CMMRD.

Thoughts For Parents and Families

On Being
Written on Friday 25th January, 2019 at 19:33

Right in the middle of
so relieved to be alive
and guilty for not being
grateful about it sooner
and upset at the lengths
I've had to go to
in order to be fixed.

And also, always:

Afraid of being afraid
of being afraid of fearing
that fearing that I feared
being afraid of being afraid
that I was afraid of fearing
afraid of being afraid of being
– afraid of being.

Well then, please wait.
I may walk a long way.
There are other things
I do not have yet.
Recently I am more keen
to get my hands on anything;
I am very enthusiastic about
letting go a little more.
Thank you for many things to do.
Thank you for so many things I can do.

As an adult with CMMRD and someone unable to have biological children, there is a limited amount that I can say about being a parent of a child with CMMRD, and I don't want to pretend to know anything about that. However, I didn't want to write a book about CMMRD without acknowledging the pain, grief, and stress associated with being a parent of a child who has cancer or dies of cancer caused by a genetic condition. Especially as I feel privileged and humbled to be here at the age of thirty-five, albeit with three different cancers under my belt. I am still here and as Dave Dubin would say, still alive and kicking.

Guilt

Childhood cancer makes up so much of many people's CMMRD stories, even if it doesn't feel quite so relevant to my own. However, I'm sure my parents would say that at the young age of twenty-two, I was still very much their child or baby when I got cancer for the first time. And my brother was at the even younger age of sixteen when he died. While I don't know much about the topic from a parent's perspective, I do know that my parents did once say that they felt guilty that I had inherited a genetic condition from them, so I wanted to make sure I stressed in this chapter that it is absolutely not your fault, reader, or any parent's fault if your child inherited a genetic condition or disease from you. I know that may not need to be said, but parents do feel guilt even if it's illogical and even if they know it's illogical, so it only seems right to address that. *It is not your fault.* I am sure any parent reading this is keen to do anything they can for a child with CMMRD or Lynch syndrome. It's okay to

81

feel sad or scared or worried. It's also okay to enjoy happy, light moments where you can. And I would say the same to siblings – don't feel guilty if your sibling inherited a genetic condition and you didn't. Just be supportive. It's extremely unlikely that the person with CMMRD blames anyone for their genetic condition. None of us can control what we pass on.

Genetic Testing and Screening for Families

However, there are some things that we can control – for example, whether we get tested for a genetic condition and whether we go for screening. We can also control how much or how little information we want about our health conditions, and that is entirely up to the individual. Some people want to know everything it's possible to know about the disease or their surgery so that they can feel informed and in control. Some people would prefer to know the bare minimum and just let the doctors get on with what they do best. Some people may fall somewhere in between. Anything is fine – whatever way you choose to deal with it is fine. I find that in the case of CMMRD, knowledge is power. After all, if I hadn't gone to my annual gastroscopy, the doctor wouldn't have found the duodenal cancer. And if the gynaecologist hadn't referred me for further testing once he knew about my genetic condition, we wouldn't have found out about the womb cancer. So without that screening and that knowledge, I may not be here today, twice over.

Sometimes – actually all the time – I feel scared about screening, but really it's not the screening that I'm afraid of. Some of the screening is very unpleasant, but what I'm afraid of is having cancer. I used to say I hope that when they look they don't find anything, but actually, what I really hope is that there is nothing to find. If there is something there I definitely want them to find it! I want there to not be anything there to find. There is a difference, and if you're not going to screening, you could be missing something important that, if you catch it early, you might be able to do something about. Screening is not the enemy. Doctors and hospitals are not the enemy. Cancer is the enemy. Sometimes it's easy to feel like hospitals themselves are the thing causing the problem rather than trying to solve it. I know I have to fight against these feelings because of how traumatic some of my previous medical experiences have been. But screening is important and knowing that you have a genetic condition is important because if you don't know you have the condition, you'll still have it – you just won't know about it. If you don't go to screening, you might still have cancer and you just won't know about it. It's no use being in the dark. It is scary going to screening and going to hospitals, but the alternatives – cancer, its treatment, or even failure of treatment or running out of options – are far more scary. We have a difficult cross to bear and it's not fair. But we can help ourselves and families can help each other by staying vigilant, so it's important to get tested if that's what's recommended to you, and to get the screening you are offered.

Not too much is known about CMMRD and some screening is offered even though doctors aren't completely sure whether there is a risk. For example, my consultant suggested that I go to my GP to get my skin looked at. They are not sure if CMMRD carries a risk for skin cancer but they want to be vigilant and it's good that they do. Once you're in the system, your doctors can look after you. That's a good place to be, or as good as it gets when you have CMMRD.

What Do People With CMMRD Need?

So I am different

Written on Saturday 4th March, 2023 at 10:19

After Audre Lorde, The Cancer Journals: *"I am defined as other in every group I'm a part of."*

In cancer groups, I've had three different types of cancer, so I am different.
In colostomy groups, I've had an ileostomy, so I am different.
In ileostomy groups, I now have an internal pouch, so I am different.
In internal pouch groups, I have one because of bowel cancer and not IBD, so I am different.
In bowel cancer groups, my family has Lynch syndrome, so I am different.
In Lynch syndrome groups, I have CMMRD, so I am different.
In CMMRD groups, I am not a child, so I am different.

As explained in the previous chapter, it's important to get genetic testing and any screening offered to you – or to push for testing and screening if you feel your medical team is not being vigilant enough. So that is one thing that people with CMMRD can do to help themselves and that families can support. Here are a few more.

Emotional and Mental Health Support

One extremely important area is the mental health and emotional aspect of having an increased cancer risk. This is true for the entire cancer population – people are living longer with cancer, so issues around quality of life for cancer survivors are becoming more and more important. However, I feel the burden of mental health is even higher for those predisposed to cancer diagnoses. The combination of knowing you are at high risk for cancer, the stress of going to regular screenings where you may be told you have cancer, and the treatments themselves, as well as the side effects of them, all take their toll. Add to this body image issues, worries about finances and work, and the way cancer can change relationships – cancer changes everything. So it stands to reason that CMMRD has a similar effect on our mental health. Some people without a genetic predisposition may get cancer, have treatment that deals with it successfully, and go about their lives not worrying too much about recurrence or further risk. They may be discharged by their medical team. I'm not saying that people without a genetic condition don't worry about recurrence – that is absolutely not true and I'm sure I would worry about it greatly even if I didn't have CMMRD. But those of us who do have it will never be discharged by our medical teams. We will always have to go to screening. There will never be an end to the threat of cancer. Knowledge is power but it can also be a burden. So when I think about what people with CMMRD need, or what I need, the first thing I think about is psychological support. It would be difficult to shoulder this burden alone without support or someone to talk to.

Ring Theory

When thinking about families, communities and how to support each other, one very useful tool is ring theory. Ring theory was devised by Susan Silk and Barry Goldman,[10] and it dictates which way support should flow through a community. The diagram below shows this, with the person with the illness or affliction – in this case CMMRD – in the middle. Directly next to them are their nearest and dearest, such as parents and spouses. Then there are other family members or close friends, followed by acquaintances such as more distant friends, neighbours, colleagues, and so on. The idea is that we direct comfort towards the inside of the circle and "dump out". This means that those closest to the person with CMMRD are giving them comfort instead of dumping their own stress on them. Those closer to the inside of the circle should direct comfort towards the centre, dump out towards the outer circles, and not be

----

[10] Susan Silk and Barry Goldman, 'How Not to Say the Wrong Thing', Los Angeles Times, 7 April 2013, https://www.latimes.com/opinion/op-ed/la-xpm-2013-apr-07-la-oe-0407-silk-ring-theory-20130407-story.html.

dumped on by those in the outer rings. It's a useful system to remember so that everyone can be supportive towards each other during tough times.

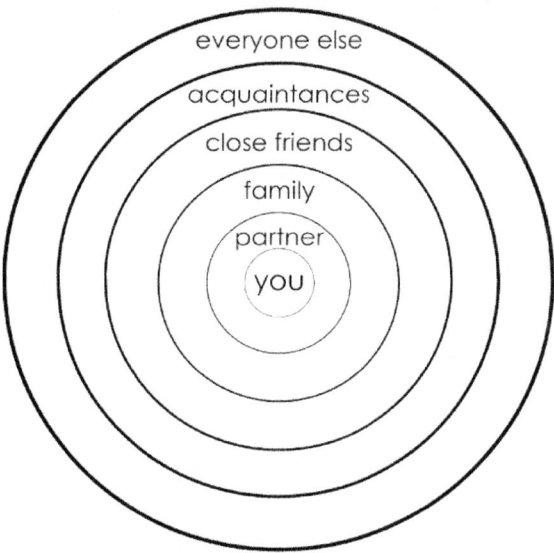

Practical Support For Appointments

Some of the most helpful things my partner does for me are taking me to my appointments, sitting with me where he can, and gathering information for me. Driving me to the hospital is helpful because it means looking for a parking space or finding out how to get to a new hospital is one less thing for me to worry about. I like to have him in my appointments because he takes an interest in understanding everything and sometimes retains information I haven't taken in. Similarly, he Googles things for me because the internet is a scary place and there's no need for me to see worrying statistics or outcomes when I'm looking for information about CMMRD, cancer, or my surgeries.

Here are ten things a partner or family member could do to support a loved one going through a CMMRD or cancer diagnosis:

- Drive them to appointments, scans and tests
- Attend appointments with them to provide emotional support, ask questions and take notes
- Google things for them
- Help them keep their medical letters and notes in order or help digitise them
- Listen to their worries and fears
- Inform the rest of the family or wider community about what is happening and answer their questions
- Do extra work around the house such as cooking and cleaning, especially if the person is going through treatment or has had surgery
- Let them rest when they need to
- Go for walks together to clear your heads or to slowly rehabilitate after surgery
- Plan nice things to do together where possible, to give them something to look forward to

Support in the Workplace

It has also been important for me to feel supported at work, and while I have been very lucky in that way, I know not everyone will have had the same experience. My previous employer paid me in full for the five months I was off work for my surgeries. I had someone to talk to about what was going on, and my team picked up my work for me and offered to help where they could and even lend a listening ear. Anyone who is dealing with a serious illness or condition benefits greatly from having that support in the workplace from both management and colleagues. However, support will look different to different people. An accommodation one person needs may not be required by someone with the same condition – and this applies to any kind of illness or disability. It's best to always be person-led rather than making any assumptions. What does the individual need?

Community

As someone with CMMRD, I want people to understand what it is like to live with a genetic condition. I know that people who don't have it will never truly be able to understand, but feeling seen and understood goes a long way towards feeling like I have that support, I have control over my situation, and I am doing something worthwhile by sharing my story and trying to help other people. So finding those opportunities to talk and be heard are important for me. Even simply someone understanding the impact of screening, and that a colonoscopy or a capsule endoscopy with bowel prep and sedation is a three-day affair rather than a quick jaunt to the hospital, feels validating. Part of feeling understood is not only explaining to those who aren't in the know but finding people who are going through similar things. This can be difficult to do, especially when you have an ultra-rare condition. It can be easy to think about all the things we don't have in common with people or all the reasons why they wouldn't understand

91

exactly what we are going through. But if we can find those with the same condition, that can unlock great understanding and feelings of community. At the very least, if it's difficult to find people in the same situations, we can try to find common ground with the people we can talk to. Surprisingly, even experiences that are entirely different from our own can provide common ground. When I talk to one of my friends, we often end up discussing either my CMMRD and cancer experiences or the death of his father. It is surprising but very validating that we find crossover within those experiences and the feelings associated with them.

Support For Children

As mentioned earlier in the book, as an adult with CMMRD and no children, I can't comment on children's needs or experiences, but I will say that what children may need will of course be different from adults. For example, they may have different emotional support and communication needs to help them (and perhaps also their siblings) understand their condition. The family may also need extra support from their school.

There's lots to think about when trying to support people of any age. If you are unsure what the person with CMMRD in your life needs, ask them! I have only covered a few issues here and everyone will be different.

Final Words of Advice

Early Morning Calling
Written on Friday 1ˢᵗ May, 2020 at 14:52

I couldn't sleep last night so I laid in bed and listened to the birds instead, and then this afternoon I thought about it and wrote this poem. This really isn't about cancer – I have tried twisting it in my head to make it that way, to find some kind of metaphor or simile but there is nothing. This is a pure poem, a happy poem, a poem of peace. And when peace is what you need, you have to create it. So why not write it? How else will you find it, if you don't look for it and give yourself a way to hold it? Maybe the answer isn't in writing about the bad, but about creating the good – because the bad already exists, and the good doesn't always magically appear. My night listening to birds appeared – but it was me who took it and made it something I could hold onto and remember, through writing. That's a way of taking control, isn't it? Control isn't just about framing your bad experiences in a way you're comfortable with, but about making space for the good things, too. And birds are good, and nature is good, and a new day is good. I want to write more poems like this one.

a jigsaw puzzle of sounds
wood pigeon with flat edges
triumphant chirps bursts

of colour on an otherwise empty
table, except they're not pieces
waiting to be moved, but creating

sound that moves and they know

94

it, organised chaos of several mating
whistles at the sun as it emerges,

come and love us, let us bask in
you, let us worship at your feet

black turns to grey turns to blue-white
haze, a new world seeping through
the crack in the curtain and instead of

lamenting lost hours, I accept,
settle in and listen, think
how often do I get to hear this?

the join between day and night
as the sky cracks and birds tumble
out of it, singing all the way down.

I hope this book has been useful for you if you have had a CMMRD diagnosis, or if your child, someone in your family, or someone else you know has CMMRD. I will leave you with eight short takeaways:

1. **Get genetic testing if it's recommended to you or if you think you're at risk.** It might just save your life or the lives of your children, or inspire someone else to get tested.

2. **Go to any screening you are offered.** Knowledge is power, and your medical team is there to help you. Scans and tests are better than the alternative.

3. **Look after your physical health.** I have a complicated relationship with advice around nutrition because I sometimes feel blamed for getting cancer by not doing everything right all the time. Nonetheless, I'll mention anyway that it is always important to have a healthy diet, exercise regularly, and get a good night's sleep.

4. **Look after your mental health.** This applies whether you have CMMRD or someone you love does. Check in on them regularly. High cancer risk is tough to deal with and even if they look fine, they might not be doing okay. You can't see what's going on inside people's heads.

5. **Find your people.** A solid community can encourage you, validate you, and help you feel understood. This can go a long way towards

keeping hold of your identity and confidently navigating the difficult terrain of CMMRD.

6. **Talk or write or create or move.** Do something you love, especially if it gives you an outlet. Try not to bottle up your feelings. Something that gives you a release, like art, sport, or telling your story, could be very helpful.

7. **There is no right or wrong way to do CMMRD.** You are not your condition. But equally, if it's embedded into your life or identity in a positive way, that's okay.

8. **Try to keep being you, even when you get lost.** Cancer and CMMRD risks take their toll but you're still in there somewhere.

Resources

Here are some online resources that may be helpful for you if you or a loved one has been diagnosed with CMMRD.

Alive and Kick'n website and podcast
aliveandkickn.org

International Replication Repair Deficiency Consortium
replicationrepair.ca

Krishnan Family Foundation, a US-based 501(c)(3) CMMRD patient advocacy organization

Lynch Syndrome UK charity
lynch-syndrome-uk.org

Private Facebook group
"CMMRD/BMMRD AWARENESS: Constitutional Mismatch Repair Deficiency"

St. Jude Children's Research Hospital webpage on CMMRD
stjude.org/disease/constitutional-mismatch-repair-deficiency.html

Acknowledgements

Thank you to my partner Peter for humouring my impulsive whims and always adding more humour to my life. Thank you to our friends, family and colleagues for always supporting us. Thank you of course to the many healthcare professionals who have been involved in my care over the years. Thank you to Dave Dubin at Alive and Kick'n for helping me open those CMMRD floodgates. And thank you to my editor and friend Christopher John Eggett for helping me not only with this book but so much of my writing over the years.

References

Abedalthagafi, Malak. 'Constitutional Mismatch
    Repair-Deficiency: Current Problems and
    Emerging Therapeutic Strategies'. *Oncotarget* 9,
    no. 83 (23 October 2018): 35458–69.
    https://doi.org/10.18632/oncotarget.26249.

Bowel Cancer UK. 'New Draft Guidance Says Aspirin
    Taken Daily Could Reduce Risk of Bowel Cancer
    for People with Lynch Syndrome'. Accessed 14
    July 2023.
    https://www.bowelcanceruk.org.uk/news-and-
    blogs/news/new-draft-guidance-says-aspirin-
    taken-daily-could-reduce-risk-of-bowel-cancer-
    for-people-with-lynch-syndrome/.

'Constitutional Mismatch Repair Deficiency'. Accessed
    8 July 2023.
    https://www.genturis.eu/l=eng/Thematic-
    disease-groups/Other-rare-
    genturis/Constitutional-Mismatch-Repair-
    Deficiency.html.

'Constitutional Mismatch Repair Deficiency Syndrome:
    MedlinePlus Genetics'. Accessed 8 July 2023.
    https://medlineplus.gov/genetics/condition/consti
    tutional-mismatch-repair-deficiency-syndrome/.

'Definition of Disability under the Equality Act 2010 -
    GOV.UK'. Accessed 7 August 2023.
    https://www.gov.uk/definition-of-disability-
    under-equality-act-2010.

'NHS England» Life-Saving NHS Test Helping to
    Diagnose Thousands with Cancer-Causing
    Syndrome'. Accessed 8 July 2023.

https://www.england.nhs.uk/2023/04/life-saving-nhs-test-helping-to-diagnose-thousands-with-cancer-causing-syndrome/.

Silk, Susan, and Barry Goldman. 'How Not to Say the Wrong Thing'. Los Angeles Times, 7 April 2013. https://www.latimes.com/opinion/op-ed/la-xpm-2013-apr-07-la-oe-0407-silk-ring-theory-20130407-story.html.

The National Lottery. 'Lotto Online Game Procedures'. Accessed 9 July 2023. https://www.national-lottery.co.uk/games/lotto/game-procedures.

'What Is a Rare Disease? - Rare Disease UK', 12 April 2018. https://www.raredisease.org.uk/what-is-a-rare-disease/.

Wimmer, Katharina, Christian P. Kratz, Hans F. A. Vasen, Olivier Caron, Chrystelle Colas, Natacha Entz-Werle, Anne-Marie Gerdes, et al. 'Diagnostic Criteria for Constitutional Mismatch Repair Deficiency Syndrome: Suggestions of the European Consortium "Care for CMMRD" (C4CMMRD)'. *Journal of Medical Genetics* 51, no. 6 (1 June 2014): 355–65. https://doi.org/10.1136/jmedgenet-2014-102284.

Printed in Great Britain
by Amazon